Women in the Renaissance

Theresa Huntley

Crabtree Publishing Company

www.crabtreebooks.com

Renaissance World

Author: Theresa Huntley
Editor-in-Chief: Lionel Bender
Editor: Kathy Middleton
Project coordinator: Kathy Middleton
Photo research: Susannah Jayes
Design concept: Robert MacGregor
Designer: Ben White
Production coordinator: Ken Wright
Production: Kim Richardson
Prepress technician: Ken Wright
Consultant: Lisa Mullins, Department of History and
  Philosophy of Science, University of Cambridge

Cover photo: Tito, Santi di (1536-1603)
  Portrait of Caterina de' Medici, Queen of France.
  Location: Uffizi, Florence, Italy
  Photo Credit : Scala / Art Resource, NY

Title page photo: Painting of the Duchess of Urbino
  by Piero della Francesca 1465.

Photographs and reproductions:
The Granger Collection, NYC/TopFoto: pages 1, 5, 6, 8, 11, 14,
  16, 20, 21, 24, 29, 30.
Topfoto: pages 4 (Luisa Ricciarini), 7 (Print Collector/HIP),
  9 (©2005 Roger-Viollet), 10 (Alinari Archives, Florence),
  12 (Seat Archive/Alinari Archives), 13 (Art Media/HIP),
  15 (©2005 Roger-Viollet) 17 (The British Library/HIP),
  18 (©2005 Roger-Viollet), 19 (©ullsteinbild), 22 (Luisa
  Ricciarini), 23 (NiccolÚ Orsi Battaglini/Alinari Archives,
  Florence, Reproduced with the permission of Opera di
  Santa Maria del Fiore), 25 (Clive Barda/PAL), 26 (The
  British Library), 27 (©2005 Roger-Viollet), 28 (Alinari
  Archives-Alinari Archive, Florence), 31 (©ullsteinbild).

This book was produced for Crabtree Publishing Company
  by Bender Richardson White.

Library and Archives Canada Cataloguing in Publication
Huntley, Theresa, 1983-
   Women in the Renaissance / Theresa Huntley.
(Renaissance world)
Includes index.
ISBN 978-0-7787-4598-3 (bound).--ISBN 978-0-7787-4618-8
(pbk.)

   1. Women--History--Renaissance, 1450-1600--Juvenile
literature.
2. Renaissance--Juvenile literature. I. Title. II. Series:
Renaissance world (St.
Catharines, Ont.)

HQ1148.H85 2010   j305.4094'09024
C2009-902426-8

Library of Congress Cataloging-in-Publication Data
Huntley, Theresa, 1983-
   Women in the Renaissance / Theresa Huntley.
   p. cm. -- (Renaissance world) Includes index.
   ISBN 978-0-7787-4618-8 (pbk. : alk. paper) --
   ISBN 978-0-7787-4598-3 (reinforced library binding : alk.
paper)
   1. Women--History--Renaissance, 1450-1600--Juvenile literature. 2. Renaissance--Juvenile literature. I. Title. II. Series.

HQ1148.H87 2010
305.4094'09031

2009016730

Crabtree Publishing Company
www.crabtreebooks.com   1-800-387-7650

Published in Canada
Crabtree Publishing
616 Welland Ave.
St. Catharines, Ontario
L2M 5V6

Published in the United States
Crabtree Publishing
PMB16A
350 Fifth Ave., Suite 3308
New York, NY 10118

Published in the United Kingdom
Crabtree Publishing
White Cross Mills
High Town, Lancaster
LA1 4XS

Published in Australia
Crabtree Publishing
386 Mt. Alexander Rd.
Ascot Vale (Melbourne)
VIC 3032

Contents

During the Renaissance, people believed that everyone could achieve greatness. But they meant every man. Women were seen as inferior to men. They were expected to be wives and mothers, were not well educated, and did not engage much in life outside the home.

Rebirth

The period from the early 1300s to the mid-1600s in much of Europe is known as the "Renaissance," a word meaning "rebirth" in French. People admired the great achievements of ancient Greece and Rome in architecture, art, literature, and science. They wanted their society to resemble these classical ideals. It was a time of prosperity, and as the population grew, **trade** increased and cities got bigger.

Social Change

In urban areas, a new social class developed in between the nobility—the upper class—and the poor farmers and laborers—the lower class. This middle class earned its money through banking or practicing a trade. Also, nobles and scholars of the time developed a belief system called **humanism** that stressed the ability of humans to do great things. Women, however, were not seen as part of this. The invention of the printing press helped spread these ideas throughout Europe.

The School of Athens *by Italian artist Raphael was painted in 1509–1511. It represents all of human knowledge by depicting important male thinkers from the past and present.*

Views of Women

Society in the Renaissance was **patriarchal** which means that men held all the power. The eldest male was the head of the family and men ran the government. People believed that women could not be in charge because they were inferior to men. This understanding of women was based on old philosophical and religious traditions.

Ancient writers believed that the smaller bone structure and skulls of women meant they were weaker and less intelligent than men. This weakness came from women's relation to Eve, the first woman in the Bible. Eve gave Adam—the first man—fruit from the Tree of Knowledge, which God had forbidden them to eat. God punished Eve so that she had to be obedient to her husband and suffer pain in childbirth. People believed that Eve passed her sinful nature and these punishments on to future women. They believed women were not capable of being great or doing much besides having children.

In his painting about poetry, Raphael showed the Greek goddesses, the Muses, who inspired men to make art, music, drama, and literature.

Stuck in the Past

Women were seen as the property of their fathers and then of their husbands. The focus of women's lives was to marry well, be good wives for their husbands, and produce male heirs. Education was considered to be wasted on women, except in the upper class, where it was seen as a pastime. In spite of these attitudes, there were some women whose accomplishments in literature, art, and politics were extraordinary.

TIMELINE

1376 Catherine of Siena helps reestablish the leaders of the Catholic Church in Rome

1405 Christine de Pisan writes *Book of the City of Ladies*

1429 Joan of Arc leads French troops to victory in the 100 Years' War with England

1492 Queen Isabella of Spain finances Christopher Columbus' voyage to the New World (the Americas)

1509 Isabella d'Este rules Mantua in northern Italy after her husband is captured by the French

1529 Louise of Savoy and Margaret of Austria negotiate the Treaty of Cambrai

1558 Queen Elizabeth I begins her 45-year reign of England

1559 Catherine de' Medici's husband, King of France, dies and she takes over as **Regent**

Women's Appearance

Women in the Renaissance were expected to be devout, obedient, modest, and beautiful. People at the time believed that a person's physical appearance reflected how good they were as a person. Ladies tried to live up to these expectations and spent a lot of time and money trying to look attractive.

In Italy, women wore elaborate braids—strands of ribbons, cords, threads, and hair woven together— instead of headdresses.
This portrait of the Duchess of Urbino, Italy, dates from 1465.

Cosmetics

The ideal woman of the time had pale skin, rosy cheeks, red lips, and blonde or reddish–colored hair. She used cosmetics to alter her appearance. The poor could not afford such luxuries and did not wear cosmetics.

Pale skin was a symbol of nobility since poorer people were forced to go outside and work in the sun, making their skin tanned. To achieve pale skin, women in England used ceruse, a skin-whitening material, and used red-colored facepaints to make their cheeks and lips rosy. Unfortunately, many of the chemicals in cosmetics, such as lead, were poisonous and caused serious health problems. It was a high price to pay for beauty.

Hairstyles

A woman's hair was a sign of her beauty and social standing. Young unmarried girls wore their hair loose. Married women in much of Europe wore veils and elaborate headdresses made of wire and mesh. Women also used chemicals and dyes to alter their hair color. They would apply common liquids like bleach or lemon juice to their hair and fan it out in the sun to change it to blonde. Others shaved their heads and bought wigs, which were often made from hair sold to wigmakers by poor women and nuns.

Undergarments

The ideal look for women was wide shoulders, narrow waists, and full hips. Rich women wore a corset to flatten the chest and make the body seem longer, and a device called a **farthingale** to make the hips look wider. It also made a dress expand to look more like a bell or a cone. Lower-class women wore a padding of loose under-dresses to make their hips look wider. For underwear, women wore lightweight dresses, but Catherine de' Medici, the wife of King Henry II of France, was one of the first women to wear drawers, or pantlike underwear. These gave women freedom to ride horses without exposing themselves.

Clothing

Women dressed as well as they could, to attract a husband and to show off their husband's wealth. Lower-class people dressed in garments made from wool, linen, and cotton. Upper-class people bought silk from Flanders (modern-day Belgium) and velvet from Spain and Italy to use as clothing material in order to display their wealth. Fabrics were brightly colored and had neat patterns of flowers or stripes. Clothing was often trimmed with lace, a luxury item imported from the cities of Venice and Antwerp. The nobility also wore rings and jewelry with diamonds and gems that were cut in new ways that allowed them to sparkle more.

Displaying Wealth

As more people in the middle class became rich, they displayed their wealth through fashion. This was especially true of women. Laws were put in place in an attempt to stop the middle class from trying to dress like nobles or royalty. These laws limited the amount middle–class people could spend on clothes as well as the types of fabrics and jewels that could be worn by them. King Henry VIII of England ruled that only royalty could wear ermine fur. Speacial tags on clothing, were also used to identify non-Christians and women of poor character. This helped insure that Christians would not be tempted to marry people deemed unsuitable.

Ladies wearing outfits for different occasions in Germany in the 1500's. The women are wearing clothes for—from left to right—church, the home, the city, and the ball.

Education

During the Renaissance, more people than ever before learned to read and write. Schools were set up to teach children basic literacy because learning and knowledge were highly valued and seen as ways to get ahead in business.

Public Education

In many cities, public elementary schools were provided for young middle- and upper-class boys whose parents could pay. There were no such schools in rural communities. In school, students learned to read and write basic Latin as well as the everyday language of their homeland, such as Italian or French. Students could go on to secondary school or attend an abacus school, which taught basic mathematics. The math school was important for the middle class because a young boy would learn skills needed to be a merchant or banker. By the late 1400s, students were reading copies of ancient Roman texts in their classes.

Private Education

Private education was a sign of wealth and importance, particularly in Venice and Florence in Italy. Upper-class people often paid tutors to instruct their sons in reading and writing, history, foreign languages, and ancient texts. Middle-class families educated their sons to increase their family's status.

If a boy knew enough Latin, he could attend university in Bologna, Padua, or Paris, and become a lawyer, theologian, or doctor.

Education of Girls

Few young girls attended elementary school. Girls did not advance far in the education system, and they were not allowed to attend university. Pleasing a husband and learning household skills were far more important for women than reading or writing. Girls were encouraged to learn spinning, sewing, and **embroidery**, and how to manage a household.

This colored woodcut image from 1510 by German artist Albrecht Dürer shows the type of classroom that young boys attended. Teachers were always men.

Tutors at Home

Lower-class girls, like lower-class boys, did not have any formal education. Middle-class girls had some opportunities for schooling. A young woman of the upper class, though, did have some formal education through tutors in the home, especially if she had brothers.

Learned Women

In northern Europe in the 1500s, people felt that the Catholic Church led by the Pope was corrupt, and they formed their own branch of Christianity called Protestantism. Protestants believed that reading the Bible and praying directly to God was the way to express faith instead of the ceremonies used by Catholics.

By the 1500s, young girls in Germany and Sweden had to go to elementary school to learn to read the Bible. In southern Europe, which was mostly Catholic, only women of higher classes and royalty were well educated. Margaret of Navarre was a famous French writer. As sister of the French king, she supported the arts and became known as the mother of the French Renaissance.

In European courts, well-educated women called courtesans provided companionship and pleasure to noblemen in exchange for financial support. A courtesan's skills in conversation, poetry, and music made her appealing to her patrons. Veronica Franco (1546-1591), a famous Venetian courtesan, even had a book of her poems published.

According to medieval legend, the young Virgin Mary was very pious and insisted that her mother, St. Anne, teach her the Bible. This statue of Mary and Anne was made in the late 1400s.

Professor Beatriz Galindo

One of the most educated women in the Renaissance was Beatriz Galindo, a Spanish woman who attended university and received a degree in Latin and Philosophy. She became a professor at the University of Salamanca in Spain and tutored the children of Queen Isabella I of Spain.

Marriage

For a Renaissance woman, the most important event of her life was her wedding day. She was expected to marry well to benefit her family's social standing and to make her husband proud.

Women as Property

In Renaissance Europe, a woman could be married as young as 13 years of age, often to a man several years or decades older than herself. Women were thought of as property. Before she married, the bride's family had to present the groom—her future husband—with a **dowry,** which was money or property that would help the couple build their home. The groom had control of the dowry, but it was insurance for the bride if her husband died. She could then use the money to support herself and her family.

Many noble or middle-class families wanted to boost their importance by making sure their daughter married into a good family. The higher the dowry, the better the marriage. Rising dowry costs in the 1400s led to some middle- and lower-class families not being able to afford to have their daughters marry. Women who worked could provide their own dowry out of their wages.

Marriage Ceremonies

Lower-class marriages were often just spoken agreements in church between men and women with no documentation or licence. Upper-class and especially royal weddings were lavish affairs, featuring a church ceremony and banquet, and elaborate clothing for the bride. They were more public and formal because the married couple and their families wanted to show their power and influence in society. Once married, the woman had to behave properly so as not to disgrace her husband. By the late 1500s, marriage contracts were common among all levels of society, including peasants.

This image shows a middle-class bride and groom in a marriage ceremony. Their respective families are present.

The Importance of Chastity

The way a woman looked and carried herself said a lot not only about her but also about her family. A wife was expected to be devout and chaste. Her chastity and virtue—how well and politely she behaved and how faithful she was—reflected on her family's honor. A woman who strayed outside of marriage damaged the reputation of her husband's family. Adultery was a serious crime in the Renaissance, punished by the courts of law.

Divorce

The Catholic Church believed that a marriage should last for life and did not allow divorce. In 1527, King Henry VIII of England wanted to divorce his wife, Catherine of Aragon, because she had not produced a son, and because he wanted to marry Anne Boleyn. He had to ask the Pope for permission to do this in order to make his next marriage valid. Pope Clement VII said no.

Henry was enraged and proceeded with his marriage to Anne anyway. The Pope

Images of the Virgin Mary marrying Joseph were popular as they showed an ideal marriage.

excommunicated Henry, which means the King was no longer a member of the Church and could not enter heaven. Henry then made himself the Head of the Church of England in 1532. His subjects had to swear loyalty to him, not the Pope. Henry's divorce from Catherine made the King of Spain very angry because he was a Catholic and Catherine was his daughter. England would later become a Protestant country. Henry's divorce shows the importance of marriage in the politics of Europe at this time.

Solidifying Spanish Power

All the kingdoms of Spain were united in 1469 when Isabella I, Queen of Castille, married Ferdinand II, king of Aragon, Sicily, Naples, Valencia, Sardinia and Navarre. The couple ruled as independent equals and Isabella's titles passed to her daughter, not her husband, at her death. Isabella famously funded Christopher Columbus's voyage of discovery to the New World in 1492, which helped to make Spain a wealthy and powerful country in the later years of the Renaissance.

Motherhood

Family was very important for people in the Renaissance, especially after the Black Death or plague of 1348. This disease killed one third of the population of Europe. Care of the family fell mostly to women. For married women, having and raising children was the major part of life.

Childbirth

Giving birth held great risk in the Middle Ages and Renaissance. Many women died in labor and many children died soon after birth. Doctors and surgeons knew very little about the way the human body works and even less about the female body, which they regarded as "less formed", than the bodies of men. Much of this information came from texts by doctors of medicine such as Antonius Guainerius (died 1450), who knew more ancient theories about female bodies than about actual female anatomy.

Although a doctor was often present during the labor of an upper-class woman, most expecting mothers, including wealthy ones, relied on midwives to deliver the baby. Midwives, though not highly regarded by doctors because they were women and not trained at medical schools, had invaluable practical experience with the birth process.

Outside Help

Since pregnancy was so difficult, many families prayed for assistance from God or from special saints who were known to perform miracles related to childbirth. These included the Virgin Mary, St. Anne, and St. Margaret. Women also used objects that were believed to possess magical powers for conception and childbirth. Wearing red coral was supposed to help fertility. Snakeskins, rabbit's milk, and diamonds were believed to prevent miscarriage. By the 1600s, when the plague was less common and medical texts became more informative, these objects were less commonly used.

This sculpture of the Birth of St. John the Baptist *from the Cathedral of Mazaro del Vallo in Sicily, Italy, shows figures in contemporary clothing and surroundings, which helped the viewer to relate to the story.*

Giving Birth to Boys

Next to health, the sex of the newborn was most important. A woman who gave her husband male heirs to carry on the family name greatly improved her family's social standing and demonstrated her worth as a woman.

Well into the 1600s, it was believed that looking at certain images could help determine the appearance and sex of a child. If women looked at images of baby boys, it was believed that this image would be "imprinted" on the child in the womb and would determine its sex. As a result, birthing objects often featured images of little boys.

Caring for Children

Traditionally, women cared for the family but royal and wealthy women often had nurses or nannies to tend to their children. Upper-class women also employed wetnurses to breastfeed their children so they did not have to. Later, this practice was frowned upon and reform movements encouraged more "motherly" behavior in upper-class women. Children produced in a marriage legally belonged to the husband in most cases. If a woman was widowed and went back to her family, her children usually had to go and live with her husband's family.

St. Margaret's story describes how she burst out of a dragon's belly unharmed by making the sign of the cross—as shown in a book from the 1400s. She is the patron saint of childbirth.

The Woman Surgeon

Alessandra Giliani was a woman from the city of Bologna, Italy, who was an assistant to a surgeon named Modino de' Luzzi. Modino wrote an important book on anatomy in 1316. Alessandra was his assistant and specialized in dissections, inventing a technique for injecting colored dye into the veins of a dissected body in order to view the blood vessels better.

Women married young and often outlived their husbands. Because they were dependent upon their husbands for money and security, becoming a widow left most of them in an uncertain position. Wealthy upper-class or royal women often stepped into their late husbands' positions and ran their families or kingdoms, but for most independence was a scary prospect in a society run by men.

Independence

A woman's dowry was often returned to her upon the death of her husband so she could support herself. A husband might also leave her in control of his wealth until their male children were able to take over. Catherine de' Medici took control of the French royal family after the death of her husband, King Henry II, until her sons grew up.

A woman could also return to her family or live with her son's family, but lower-class women whose relatives were not rich could not do this. Often, poor widows were forced into basic work of cleaning and serving in inns if any was available, and some even turned to prostitution to get by. Poverty and homelessness were real concerns. Many women begged for help.

A small picture, called a miniature, of Mary, Queen of Scots.

Twice a Widow

Mary Stuart, also known as Mary, Queen of Scots, lived from 1542 to 1587. Her life shows the difficulties faced by royal widows. She married twice and was widowed twice by the age of 24. She married again and was imprisoned by the Scottish nobility to force her to give her throne to her son. Seeking help from her Protestant cousin Queen Elizabeth I, she fled to England but was imprisoned because Elizabeth feared that Catholics in England believed Mary to be their rightful ruler. She was executed in 1587 for her connection with assassination plots.

Mourning the Husband

As a widow, a woman was expected to look after her husband's memory and her family's honor by entering a period of mourning. This could last for the rest of her life.

A widow showed her grief through her clothing, wearing a simple, black, high-collared dress and a small pointed veil on the top of her head, called a "widow's peak." Widows wore modest jewelry that represented mourning, such as black coral and pearls. They were encouraged to dress simply, but not in poor quality clothing since this would reflect negatively on their late husbands.

Proper Behavior

The independence of widows was a cause for concern in the Renaissance. Many middle- and upper-class husbands left instructions in their wills for their wives' behavior and dress.

This three-paneled altarpiece shows Catherine de' Medici in mourning. Her husband died in 1559 from a head wound by a lance.

Spanish author Juan Luis Vive's book on the proper conduct of women said that a widow should grieve her husband, dedicate her life to prayer and charity, and never remarry.

Many women did remarry, often for financial or political reasons, or at their family's demand. If a widow remarried, her children could be raised by her late husband's family. Other women took up a kind of religious life. Groups of widows attached themselves to a monastery or church and performed acts of charity in the community but they did not have to live like nuns or take religious vows or promises. The behavior of men who lost their wives was never given as much attention or concern.

Women at Home

During the Renaissance, the home was the woman's responsibility. Men dealt with the public life of the city or farming community, and women looked after the private life of the family and the home.

Construction of the House

Families who lived outside of large cities worked as farmers. In farming communities, the lower-class home was very small. The kitchen was the most important part of the house. It was where family members ate and where some of them slept in order to be closer to the fire used for cooking and heating.

Lower-class people in cities had smaller homes in crowded neighborhoods, and often rented rooms from landlords. Houses were built very narrow and deep allowing for more homes to be built on one street. Tradesmen such as shoemakers and tailors often each had their workshop in the street-level story of their house. The upper story was where the family lived.

Upper-class homes were very similar, although the main story was more open and considered a public space even though there was no shop. Visitors would enter through the main gate or door and the inner courtyard was often visible from the street. A family's servants lived in the house.

Lower-Class Women in the Home

In farming communities, women were responsible for tending the children, sweeping the floors, laundry, washing cooking utensils, and preparing and cooking the family's food. They had to carry water from nearby streams to the home in large jugs, and they did their laundry in the streams. Sometimes this could be hazardous as many women did not know how to swim. Women also combed and spun wool and made clothing for the family.

The Medici family were bankers but were in the highest social class of the republic of Florence. Their house, seen here, is divided into three stories. The arches on the lowest story were once large windows so people could see inside. The women of the house lived in the top storey.

Daily Shopping

In a city, the responsibilities of a lower-class married woman were similar except that she had to go and buy meat and bread every day because butchering and baking in urban homes was very difficult. There was less room for food preparation, and an oven in a small house could be very dangerous.

Nobles and Royals

Upper-class women were also supposed to make the home a welcome and happy place for their husbands. They were responsible for all of the domestic jobs such as laundry, cooking, and cleaning. But middle- and upper-class families could afford servants to actually carry out those duties. Middle-class wives whose husbands were tradesmen or businessmen would have a few servants and would do some of the work themselves. Noble and royal women supervised the workings of the household, which were entirely performed by a large number of servants. Upper-class mothers did not look after their children but hired nannies to do this. These women were free to enjoy more leisure. They practiced needlepoint or embroidery and, if they were well educated, read or wrote poetry or letters.

The Virgin Mary practices needlepoint while her husband, St. Joseph, sands a table. This is a Spanish book illumination from around 1450.

Hiding of the Upper Class

Women of noble families remained inside the home most of the time. They left the home only for church services on Sunday, so dressing up for church was a big event. It was believed that keeping women indoors would limit their contact with other men and so avoid affairs and illegitimate children, and protect the family line. One traveler to Venice in the 1500s said that he was looking for the famous beauties of Venetian nobility, but could not see any of them!

Women at Work

The life of a woman was very different depending on whether she lived in the country or in the city, and whether she was poor or wealthy. Generally, wealthy or noble women did not work at all.

Country Work

Although most work on farms required great physical strength, women did help their farmer husbands or worked under contract for the landowner. Women raised the children and looked after the home and the family garden. They also weeded the crops in the spring, reaped corn in the harvest, and collected loose grain after harvesting. If the family had livestock, women would help raise the tiniest or orphaned cows or lambs. Women were mainly responsible for milking cattle, the production of butter and cheese, the care of chickens, and the gathering of eggs. In areas where grapes were grown, harvesting and crushing grapes for wine was done by both sexes equally.

If women were hired to do a job during the harvest season, they were often paid less than a male would receive. But in helping her husband, a woman contributed to the financial situation of her family.

Taking Over

There were greater job opportunities for women in cities. Women could not apprentice in the **trade guilds,** but guilds did allow widows to carry on their husband's business after his death. Wives often helped their husbands' with their business, particularly as shopkeepers.

A scene of rural life by Flemish painter Jan Brueghel (1568-1625.) Women took part in most of the activities.

Finding Employment

In the Middle Ages, there were records of women working as butchers, bakers, tailors, and dyers. Places such as the German city of Cologne had separate women's guilds for yarn-makers, spinners of gold thread, and silk-weavers. But as the population of Europe grew after the great plague of 1347, there were more men available for work and women were forced into simpler jobs.

Most women who worked for a wage found employment in domestic service or as a server in an inn or tavern. Women could enter domestic service at a very young age. Families too poor to pay for a dowry for their daughters often gave them to a wealthy family to work as a servant until they married. The wealthy family would often pay the girl wages and cover her dowry. Women also found employment as wetnurses and as midwives.

Freedom of the Lower Class?

It was considered a sign of wealth and prestige if the women of a family did not work. But in many ways, lower-class women had greater freedom than those in the upper class. Working women were allowed to leave the house more, if only for shopping or to get firewood and water. Yet women who had to work to support themselves or their families also had to raise the children and do the basic domestic duties around their own houses. Women did men's work, but men did not do housework or look after the children.

Prostitution

Prostitution—a woman offering pleasure to men for money—was common, and many women who could not find jobs worked out of their homes, or in brothels, as prostitutes. In the upper class, some educated women became courtesans and provided pleasure but also companionship to their noble or royal patrons. Courtesans were valued for their conversation, charm, and artistic talents in poetry and music. Some achieved great power at court, such as Diane de Poitiers, the courtesan of King Henry II of France, who influenced the king's political decisions.

A drawing from the 1500s of a middle-class woman from the city (on the left) and a lower-class woman from the country (on the right.)

While it was preferable for a woman to become a wife to help her family's interests, it was also acceptable for women to serve in the religious community. Women could not become priests, bishops, or cardinals, but they could enter religious life as a nun.

Religious Orders

In the Middle Ages and the Renaissance, many types of religious communities were created. They focused on chastity, poverty, and obedience as a way to copy and become closer to Jesus Christ. To become a member of an **order,** a person would have to take vows and promise to obey the guidelines for living in the religious community.

Male and female members of the order did not live together. Male members, or monks, lived in monasteries while female members, or nuns, lived in convents. Women who did not want to live in the convent or who were widowed could participate in the religious community as a **tertiary.**

Life in the Convent

A girl would enter a convent as early as five years of age or as late as 20. Her parents would have to give money to the convent in order to pay for her food and upkeep. This was a kind of dowry, and it was thought that when a girl entered a convent, she became a bride of Christ.

As a nun, a girl chose to live a life of poverty, prayer, and seclusion instead of marriage. Living in a convent was regarded as safer than getting pregnant and risking death during childbirth. Daily life focused on attending religious services, prayer, reading, writing, and even singing in the choir.

French manuscript from 1300 showing nuns celebrating Mass and walking through the convent.

New Opportunities

In convents, women could get an education. For centuries, knowledge was kept in the libraries of monasteries and convents. Monks and nuns carefully copied and translated ancient religious, medical, and philosophical texts in the scriptoria, or writing rooms. Nuns also illustrated many of these **manuscripts** and wrote their own poetry and religious texts. Women could also take up important jobs within the convent, becoming head administrators or **abbesses.**

Non-Christians

People who were not Christian were often persecuted, or treated badly, by the Church as **heretics.** Jews and Muslims in Europe were expelled from such countries as Spain and England, subjected to violence, or forced to convert to Christianity. Marriage between people of different religions was not permitted. Christian women who took part in activities thought to be heretical by the Catholic or Prostestant Church could also face an accusation of witchcraft. Such women were often middle-aged or elderly and lived on their own. Witches were believed to make potions and spells to make people sick, insane, or fall in love. The punishment for witchcraft was burning at the stake or hanging.

Doctors of the Church

In 1970, Pope Paul VI named St. Catherine of Siena and St. Teresa of Avila the first female Doctors of the Church. The title was given to people who made significant contributions to the Catholic Church. They were remarkable women who helped reform and promote Catholicism. St. Catherine was a nun of the Dominican order who worked to bring the Pope back to Rome during his displacement in France in the 1300s. St. Teresa was the founder of the Discalced or Barefoot Carmelite Order in Spain and a writer who inspired many religious reforms, or changes, in Spain in the 1500s.

A portrait of St. Teresa of Avila from 1562.

Female Saints

The main religion of Europe in the Renaissance was Christianity. Christians worship one God and believe in the teachings of Jesus Christ. The main Christian church was the Catholic Church until the 1500s, when new Christian churches began to emerge. The worship of saints was a big part of being Catholic.

The Worship of Saints

Saints played a major role in everyday life during the Renaissance. A saint was a person who had died and was believed to have gone to heaven for doing something miraculous, for dying for their faith in Christ, or for founding or reforming a monastic order.

When the altarpiece of the Virgin in Glory was painted by Italian artist Duccio in 1311, it was paraded around the streets of Siena in Italy.

People prayed to saints for help with their lives, believing that these holy people would direct the request to God and ensure a favorable outcome. In 1260, a man named Jacobus da Voragine wrote a book called *The Golden Legend* that listed all the saints and their biographies. It was so popular that hundreds of copies of it were printed and sold in Europe in the 1400s. Each day of the year was designated as a Saint's Day.

Women and Female Saints

In their sermons, many Renaissance preachers praised the saints as role models for good Christians and as sources of help for people in trouble. St. Margaret of Antioch was an important saint for women because she was the **patron saint** of childbirth. Giving birth held great risk, and she was believed to give great help to women in labor.

Showing One's Thanks

Women prayed to St. Margaret for their health and the health of their children. If they received an answer to their prayers, they left objects of devotion called ex votos, often in the shape of babies, at her altar or commissioned artwork featuring the saint. As a result of women's special devotion to her, St. Margaret was one of the most frequently represented saints in Renaissance art.

The Virgin Mary

The most important of all the female saints was the Virgin Mary. Christians believe that she was the woman whom God chose to be the mother of his son, Jesus. In the Renaissance, people believed that Mary was the perfect woman. Girls and women tried to copy her by being pious, humble, and good mothers.

Mary was very close to Jesus so people prayed to her for help with their problems more than any other saint. In Northern Europe, people saw the worship of saints and Mary as a sign of the corrupt Catholic Church. It was one of the factors leading to the development of Protestantism. Protestants did not believe in praying to saints but only to God.

Mary Magdalen and Savonarola's Florence

In the 1490s in Florence, a passionate and popular monk named Girolamo Savonarola preached about the end of the world and the evils of vanity and wealth. In 1497, he and his followers staged a "Bonfire of the Vanities," in which they burned objects believed to be a sign of immorality such as cosmetics, paintings of anything non-Christian, and tarot cards. He told people to model themselves after Mary Magdalen, a reformed prostitute and penitent who lived for 30 years in the wilderness clad only in her hair. Although he was popular, he was executed for disobeying the Pope.

Mary Magdalen was an important saint in the Renaissance. She was the patron saint of prostitutes and reformed sinners. This statue of her from 1454 is by Italian sculptor Donatello.

The Catholic Church responded to this criticism by organizing a large council, called the Council of Trent, to reform the corruption in the Church. After this, the Church began controlling the worship of saints and their depiction in art, but Mary was still very popular and important and the Church still regarded her as the perfect woman.

Extraordinary Women

During the Renaissance, it was difficult for a woman to earn respect or praise outside the home. Yet some women of the time made extraordinary achievements.

The General

During the 100 Years' War between England and France, an 18-year-old peasant girl, Joan of Arc, convinced the French king to let her lead his army against the English. Joan claimed that she was guided by God to lead France to victory. She dressed as a man in full armor, and led the French to an amazing victory at Orléans in 1429. She was captured a year later by the English and burned at the stake as a heretic but was later made a saint and became a national heroine of France.

The Pirate Queen

The O'Malley clan of Ireland was known for its sailing skill, its trade with Scotland and Spain, and for opposing the English. Grace O'Malley first learned to sail by sneaking on board her father's ship and eventually commanded three ships and 200 men as a sea captain. She was rumored to have fallen in love with a shipwrecked man who was killed by the McMahon family. Grace retaliated by burning their ships, killing the men responsible, and capturing their castle.

She and her second husband plundered enemy communities and ships and resisted English control of their realm. When her sons were taken prisoner by Richard Bingham, the English governor of Ireland, Grace appealed to Queen Elizabeth I of England. In a famous meeting, Elizabeth granted the release of Grace's son and endorsed Grace's position and seafaring lifestyle as a pirate in Ireland.

When St. Joan led the troops, she cut her hair and dressed as a man to help the army think of her as a leader and not a woman.

La Malinche

In 1519 in Mexico, a 14-year old slave girl was given to the Spanish conquistador Hernán Cortés. The girl, called Doña Marina or La Malinche (noble captive,) spoke the Mayan and Aztec languages, and quickly learned Spanish. La Malinche worked for Cortés as a translator during his conquest of the Aztec Empire of Mexico.

La Malinche was key in convincing other native groups of Mexico to unite with the Spanish to defeat the Aztecs, and told Cortés about a plot to ambush the Spanish. Although some mondern–day Mexicans consider La Malinche to have been a traitor, many people, including people of her own time, take note of her strength and intelligence.

The Pope's Daughter

Although marriage and children were not permitted for men in the Church, Cardinal Rodrigo Borgia, who later became Pope Alexander VI, had a daughter, Lucrezia Borgia. She was very influential during her father's reign as Pope.

Lucrezia was a papal secretary, governor of the Italian region of Spoleto, and had a hand in her father's political plots. He and other leaders in Europe sought to make alliances through the marriage of Lucrezia. She married Giovanni Sforza, of the ruling family of Milan, Italy. When her father sought a stronger alliance with the Italian city of Naples, he annulled Lucrezia's marriage to Giovanni and she married a relative of the former king of Naples, Alfonso of Aragon.

Alfonso was later murdered. It was rumored that Lucrezia's brother or father had ordered his death and that she took part in it because the Borgia family was now allied to France,

an enemy of Naples. She was then made to marry Alfonso d'Este, son of the Duke of Ferrara, Italy. When her father died in 1503, Lucrezia's life calmed and she became a promoter of the arts in Ferrara.

This opera singer is performing the famous opera about Lucrezia Borgia. The opera is based on the play by French writer Victor Hugo.

As with most professions, artists and writers in the Renaissance were men. But within this time period, several women became famous authors and painters. Their numbers increased as more women than ever before had access to education and training for these careers.

Professional Difficulties

There were very few women artists in the Renaissance because artists apprenticed at a master's studio, and it was not considered proper for women to leave their homes and enter workshops. Most women who became artists had a father or husband who was also an artist and had a studio that they could work in.

Even then, it was not proper for women to look at nude models, so they could not develop the same skill in painting and sculpting the human figure as men. Even if a woman artist achieved success, she was considered to be masculine, or a man in a woman's body.

Women of Words

Women writers also had limited training and education. In religious communities, a monk or friar often had to check the work of a female writer in order for it to be taken seriously. Writing did not require working in a studio, so women authors could work on their own from home.

Letter writing was a common form of expression for women, and many noble ladies exchanged their thoughts with men in the 1500s in this way. Vittoria Colonna, for example, wrote letters and poems to the famous Italian artist Michelangelo. Vittoria was a noted female poet who knew many other writers in Rome and Venice.

A manuscript illustration of Christine de Pisan at her desk.

Famous Women Artists

The Italian painter Sofonisba Anguissola was the daughter of a wealthy gentleman and, surprisingly, **apprenticed** in a workshop. She became an internationally known artist, traveling to Spain to paint portraits of the royal court in the mid 1500s.

Properzia de' Rossi is one of the few known female sculptors of early modern Italy. She started her career by carving peach pits and eventually worked with marble. This would be difficult for a woman to do because sculpting required considerable upper body strength to use a hammer and chisel.

Novelists and Poetesses

Hélisenne de Crenne was the pen name of Marguerite Bret, a French novelist in the mid 1500s. She wrote three novels and partially translated the classical text, *The Aeneid*, by Virgil. Another famous female French writer, was Louise Labé. In 1555, she published a collection of love poems inspired by the Italian poet Petrarch, and another text called the *Debate of Folly and Love*. It was a widely–published and well-read book. She was

called "the Beautiful Rope-Maker" because of her husband's profession and she enjoyed a great deal of freedom in her marriage. Her wit, charm, and independence lead many to call her "unwomanly" and to accuse her of being a crossdresser or a courtesan.

This illustration for the publication of Louise Labé's book, Debate of Folly and Love, *dates to 1762, showing how long her work was popular.*

An Early Feminist Writer

Christine de Pisan (1383-1434) was a writer educated in a royal court where her father worked before his death. Widowed by the age of 24, Christine wrote ballads for members of court to support her family. She was Europe's first professional woman writer. By 1405, she had completed her most successful book, *The Book of the City of Ladies,* in which she outlines the contributions of women to society and emphasizes education as a way for women to fight their unfair treatment by men.

Women in Poetry and Art

Poetry and art were very important parts of Renaissance society. Women were often the subjects of poetry and of many artworks of the period. Just as now, when images of famous women in magazines, books, and on television reflect how people think of women and the way they look, the literature and paintings of the Renaissance defined the standards of female beauty.

The Importance of Beauty

In the Renaissance, people believed physical beauty reflected the goodness of a person's soul. Men and women devoted a great deal of time and energy making themselves look attractive. This was especially important for women because a woman's beauty helped secure a good husband and a successful marriage.

Petrarch and the Feminine Ideal

Francesco Petrarch was an important poet of the mid 1300s. His poems inspired generations of writers including William Shakespeare in England. He wrote 366 poems about his unfulfilled love for Laura, a woman whom he had seen once and perhaps had met, but who might also never even have existed.

The collection of these poems was called the *Canzoniere*, or Songbook. It was immensely popular and influenced the way people looked at, wrote about, and painted women. Petrarch focused on Laura's chastity, virtue, and goodness, which was reflected in her beautiful face and body. The poet praised Laura's beautiful features: her golden hair, rosy cheeks, and ivory skin. Paintings of the time also showed women having these desirable features.

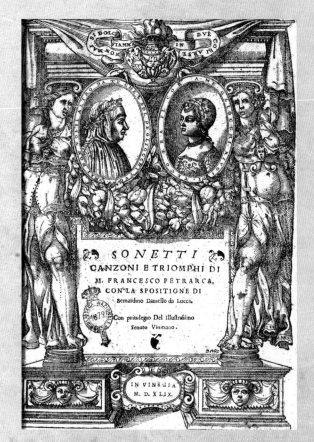

Title page of Petrarch's Sonnets, Venetian *edition, 1549. Although only a few dozen copies of Petrarch's* Songbook *existed after his death, by the early 1500s, owning a "pocket Petrarch" or small copy of the poems was very common and desirable.*

The Artist's Brush

When people heard poems or saw paintings about beautiful women, they appreciated the beauty of the women represented. But they also praised the poet and the artist for their ability to make such wonderful imagery. The more beautiful the poem or the painting, the more the poet or artist was liked.

By the 1500s, the image of the beautiful, nude woman became a standard type of painting and a way for an artist to show his talent. The Venetian artist of the early to mid1500s called Titian was famous for painting large-scale images of a nude woman. Botticelli painted nude women in many of his works. Leonardo da Vinci, the most famous Renaissance man, is best-known for the Mona Lisa, a painting he made in 1503 showing a beautiful, thoughtful woman.

The Portrait of Laura

Petrarch's friend Simone Martini (1280-1344) painted a picture of Laura, perhaps for Petrarch. The painting does not survive, but Petrarch wrote two poems about it. He praises Simone's ability to paint Laura's beauty although he complains that the painting is frustrating to look at because it does not speak to him. In his poetry, Petrarch describes Laura's voice, which a painting cannot do. In this way, Petrarch suggests that poetry is better than art at depicting beauty.

Italian artist Parmigianino was influenced by Petrarch. In his Madonna with the Long Neck *(1536-40), shown above, he focused on the long neck of Mary, which was another part of a woman's beauty that was often praised.*

Women Who Ruled

By the end of the Renaissance, there were women rulers who were well respected by their people, whatever their class and beliefs. These women challenged the common view of females in society and changed the face of Europe for centuries after. Some are now famous in history.

Republics and Courts

Republics such as the city of Florence were democratic—they were governed based on the idea of everyone being equal. Women in those societies that were based on a **court** system, with a king, queen, or head of state, often had more rights. In a democracy, people who could vote had power—and women could not vote. In a court system, upper-class women at least could inherit wealth, were more educated, and were regarded as "better" than lower-class men or women because of their noble blood.

Isabella d'Este was a noblewoman from Italy known for her intellect and her patronage of famous painters such as Leonardo da Vinci. Her husband, Federigo Gonzaga, was captured in 1509 and imprisoned for three years, leaving Isabella to rule the Italian city of Mantua in his place and again after his death. She made Mantua an important city.

Royalty

Royal or noble titles such as king, duke, and sir, passed from father to son. If a man had no male heirs, his daughter could be named queen or the head of the state. If she married, she lost her position and much of her power to her husband.

The reign of Queen Elizabeth I is known as the Golden Age of England.

Queen of England

Queen Elizabeth I of England never married because she did not want her country ruled by another European power. She had inherited the throne from her sister, Queen Mary I, whose marriage to Philip II of Spain, a Catholic, proved unpopular. Elizabeth is remembered for making England a Protestant country, supporting William Shakespeare and other writers, and defeating the Spanish Armada in 1588. She declared, "I have the body of a weak and feeble woman, but I have the heart and stomach of a king."

Regents

A woman could also rule as a regent if her husband died and her children were too young to run the country. Catherine de' Medici of France had little power when her husband the king was alive, but as a widow she ruled France as regent for their son. A woman could also be given the office of regent. After she was widowed twice, Margaret of Austria's father, the Holy Roman Emperor Maximillian, appointed her regent of the Netherlands for her nephew. She helped negotiate peace with Louise of Savoy, which temporarily ended hostility between Spain, Germany, and France.

Status of Women

In the upper class, noble blood made women more respectable in the eyes of men and education gave women more opportunities. But throughout society, women were still seen as less important than men. Women still had a long way to go to achieve equality.

The Ladies' Peace

After she became a widow at 19, the French Duchess Louise of Savoy negotiated the marriage of her son Francis to the daughter of the French King Louis XII. When Francis became king, Louise was his advisor and regent during his absence at war. She also negotiated the Treaty of Cambrai, with her sister-in-law, Margaret of Austria. This ended fighting between France, Germany, and Spain in 1529. The treaty is called the "Ladies' Peace" because of the involvement of these two women.

Isabella d'Este, seen here in a portrait by Leonardo da Vinci, was known as the "First Lady of the World."

Further Reading and Web Sites

Carolyn Meyer. *The Tudor Women Boxed Set: Mary, Bloody Mary/Beware, Princess Elizabeth/ Doomed Queen Anne/Patience, Princess Catherine.* Houghton Miffin Harcourt, 2006.

Raphael Jacquemin. *Medieval and Renaissance Fashion.* Dover Publications, 2007.

Vicki León. *Outrageous Women of the Renaissance.* John Wiley and Sons, 1999.

Renaissance Connection: www.renaissancecollection.org
Exhibits Collection—Renaissance: www.learner.org/interactives/renaissance
Elizabethan Era: www.elizabethan-era.org.uk

Glossary

abbess Woman in charge of a community of nuns

apprentice Person who studies and learns skills of a trade from a master

court The home, employees, and close followers of a noble, king, or queen

dowry Money or property brought by a bride, or her family, to her husband on their marriage

embroidery Decorating cloth with patterns of thread

excommunicate Officially ban someone from the Church

farthingale Hooped petticoat or circular pad of fabric worn worn by women under their skirts

heretic A person whose beliefs or opinions go against the Church

humanism Belief in the importance of humans and their potential for greatness

manuscript Book or document written by hand and not printed

order Society of monks, priests, or nuns who live according to religious and social regulations

patriarchy System of society or government in which family wealth and power is passed down through men in the family

patron saint Protecting or guiding saint of a person, group of people, or place

regent A person who steps in to lead a country because the monarch or head of state is too young, too sick, or absent

republic State in which power is held by the people and their elected representatives

tertiary Means "third" in Latin and refers to people who work in religious communities without taking the vows of chastity and poverty

trade The business of buying and selling goods

trade guild Association of craftsmen or merchants who practice the same trade

Index

Printed in China — CT

DATE DUE

GAYLORD | | PRINTED IN U.S.A.